The
Greater
Horseshoe
Bat

Roger Ransome

BLANDFORD PRESS
Poole · Dorset

Contents

Illustration Credits

Cover Sdeuard C. Bisserôt; E. F. Addis pages 27, 31; S. Bisserôt 7, 10, 14, 15, 18, 19, 30, 38; M. Clark 3; D. Corke 43; B. Hawkes 11, 22; P. Morris 39, 42; P. Racey frontispiece; R. Ransome 2, 6, 11, 23, 26, 27, 29, 31, 39.

Picture Editors Michael Clark   David Corke

Art Work Michael Clark   Roger Ransome

First published in Great Britain in 1980 by Blandford Press in association with The Mammal Society.

Copyright © 1980 Blandford Press Ltd
Link House, West Street
Poole, Dorset BH15 1LL

ISBN 0 7137 0986 3

British Library Cataloguing in Publication Data

Ransome, Roger
  The greater horseshoe bat.
  1. Rhinolophidae – Juvenile literature
  2. Mammals – Great Britain – Juvenile literature
  I. Title   II. Mammal Society
  599'.4   QL737.C58

Printed in Great Britain by Purnell & Sons Ltd, Paulton (Bristol) and London

Introduction

There are about fourteen different kinds of bats found in the British Isles, but several of them are very rare. They range from the tiny pipistrelle weighing about 4 g to the noctule which is the largest at 25 g lean weight. Both of these bats store a lot of fat before they hibernate, and so increase their weight considerably in late September and October. All British bats feed upon insects.

Bats are not at all easy to observe at close quarters. They hide in narrow crevices in trees, buildings or caves, and usually are seen only as they emerge to feed at dusk. As a result few people see them, even though some kinds are quite common.

The greater horseshoe bat is one of the largest of the bat species. It is slightly smaller than the noctule. Both bats have a similar wingspan, but whereas the noctule flies high in the sky and makes a high pitched squeak, the greater horseshoe flies close to the ground or vegetation, and is silent. It is a rare bat and is unlikely to be seen unless a known haunt is watched carefully at dusk, and it soon disappears into the undergrowth.

Description

In Britain it is only called the greater horseshoe bat. Its scientific, or latin, name is *Rhinolophus ferrumequinum*. 'Ferrum' means iron, and 'equinum' means horse; hence the horseshoe part is indicated. This name comes from the unusual shape of the nose, which has a leaf-like outgrowth around the nostrils. Only the lesser horseshoe bat, *Rhinolophus hipposideros,* has the same kind of nose among the British bats. All other types have normal noses and an earlet, or tragus, inside the ear. Horseshoe bats have no earlet.

All bats throughout the world belong to the mamma-

Frontispiece
Face view of a greater horseshoe bat hanging up. Note its large ears, small eyes and also the nose leaf which gives the bat its name.

1

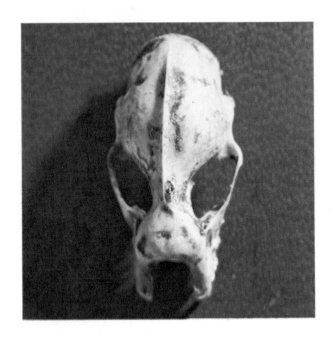

Bat skull from above. Note the large gap in the upper jaw where the front teeth (incisors) are missing.

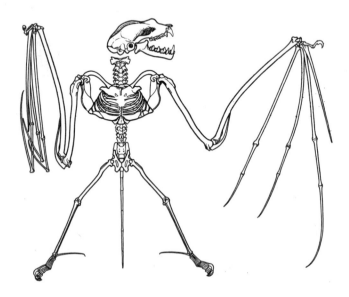

Skeleton of greater horseshoe bat.

A single bat in hibernation. It hangs upside down, held by its toenails which hook into a tiny crevice in the rock. No effort is needed to stay there.

lian order Chiroptera, which means a 'hand wing'. Horseshoe bats belong to the family Rhinolophidae.

The greater horseshoe bat is called 'le Grande Rhinolophe fer à cheval' in France, and 'der Grossen Hufeisennase' in Germany.

It has a wingspan of about 35 cm, and its forearm length is from 5.2-5.9 cm in fully grown animals. Females are very slightly larger than males. Live bats can weigh from 13.4-34 g in Britain, depending upon the age, sex and time of year. The heaviest records come from adult females in October, just before hibernation, and just before giving birth in July.

When flying, it can only be recognised definitely with the help of an ultrasonic receiver, or 'bat detector'. This is a special instrument which picks up the very high sounds the bat makes, which we cannot hear, and turns them into ones we can. It has a dial, like a radio, which can be tuned to 83 kilohertz so that it picks up the greater horseshoe bat's voice. It makes quite a musical note, whereas other species will not be picked up, or only a faint click is heard. Lesser horseshoes use an even higher sound at about 119 kilohertz. Many bats use these very high sounds for navigating in the dark.

If hibernating bats are found in caves or other places, the horseshoe bats are easily recognised since they look like black plums. They hang free from contact with the wall or ceiling, except at their toes whose claws hook into the tiniest crack. They wrap their black wings around their body unless they are part of a group, or cluster. Other bats fold their wings tightly along their forearms, and grip the walls with their thumbs as well as their feet.

The size difference between greater and lesser horseshoes is so great that it is easy to tell them apart. The lesser is about the size of an adult's thumb, or the end of a teaspoon, and the greater is the size of the end of a

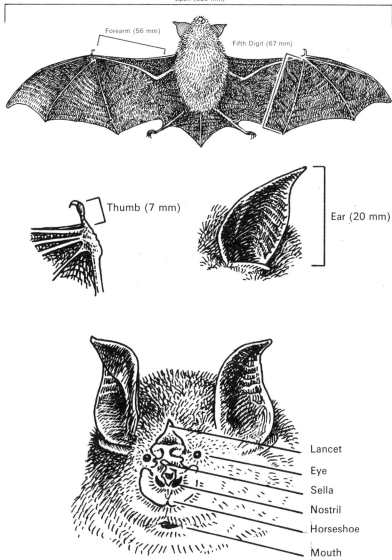

Span (350 mm)

Forearm (56 mm)

Fifth Digit (67 mm)

Thumb (7 mm)

Ear (20 mm)

Lancet

Eye

Sella

Nostril

Horseshoe

Mouth

Fig. 1 *External structure of a greater horseshoe bat, with dimensions and weights.*

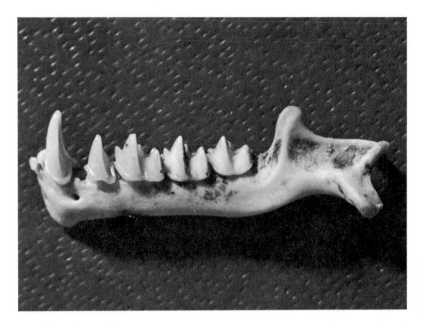

Side view of a lower jaw. The small incisors, large canines (dog teeth) and chewing teeth are typical of insect-eating mammals.

Canine teeth removed from the jaws. They are used to pierce the tough skeletons of large insect prey, especially those of beetles.

A large cluster of bats hibernating in a disused limestone mine in January. Over two hundred bats are present in this photograph. Most of them are tightly pressed together.

tablespoon. There is no need to wake them up to find out. In fact it is illegal to disturb a greater horseshoe, as it is protected by the Conservation of Wild Creatures and Wild Plants Act of 1975. Only licensed persons can wake them up for serious studies.

If the skeleton of a bat is found, the skull is the best guide to the owner. A greater horseshoe bat skull is 2.1-2.3 cm long, with a large pair of swellings behind the opening to the nose.

The skeleton shows great differences from that of a normal land mammal, such as a shrew or mouse. The forearm, hand bones and fingers are very long, except for the thumb which is the only finger with a claw. A double layer of strong thin skin is stretched over the hand and finger bones, and it is also supported by the rather weak legs and the tail. The skin has blood vessels and a set of elastic fibres to give strength. The feet are small, but have a set of five long curved claws on each one. They make useful combs for grooming the fur, as well as for gripping onto a crack in the wall when it rests, or hibernates. A suspended bat is rather like a coathanger on a rail. No effort is needed to stay there, so during hibernation the muscles are inactive.

Young bats grow very quickly, and even the babies born in July are fully grown by the time they enter caves to hibernate in October. They can only be recognised from older bats by their greyish fur, and gently tapering finger joints. Older bats have buff brown fur, and rather knobbly finger joints. Very old bats tend to have fur of a deeper, chestnut colour.

Although they grow to full size very quickly, these bats take a long time to become sexually mature. Males are two or three years old before the testes can be seen as white patches in the groin. Females generally give birth at the age of three years, and grow two small flaps of skin, called false teats, in the groin. These act as dummies for the baby bats when they are not suckling from the true teats, which are on the chest.

The teeth are normal for mammals which eat insects. The front teeth (incisors) are small, and one is missing from each side of the upper jaw. The dog teeth (canines) are large and pointed, and the chewing teeth (premolars and molars) have sharp spikes for chopping up the insect prey.

The lower jaws are only weakly joined at the front. The milk teeth are tiny and useless, and are usually lost before birth. The permanent teeth grow as soon as the baby is born. As the bat grows older its teeth wear, especially the canines. Serious wear is normally only noticeable in very old bats, such as those over sixteen years of age.

Like other bats the greater horseshoe has very large strong chest muscles for flight, and a large heart to feed them with blood when necessary. The stomach is very large as well, and can take nearly 5 g, or 25% of the body weight of insects at one meal. In autumn fat is stored for energy supplies in hibernation. Some of the fat is brown, and this type is used to make heat when the bat wakes up from hibernation. This happens every few days.

The weight of a bat depends upon its age, sex and time of year, as mentioned before. All ages are heaviest in October, and lightest in April and May. At any one time of the winter, first year bats are the lightest, and adult females are the heaviest. All other ages and sexes weigh somewhere in between.

Distribution

The greater horseshoe bat is found in south western regions of England and Wales, in north western France, across southern Europe, the middle East and northern Africa, central Asia and Japan.

*Greater horseshoe bats in flight.
The top photograph in particular
shows details of wing structure
and veining on wings.*

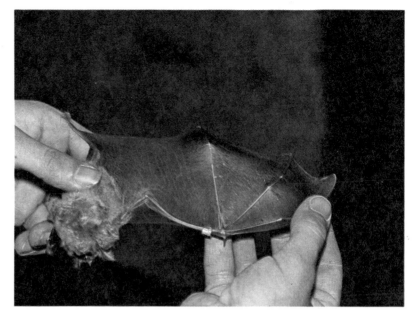

Wing of a bat spread out to show its structure, and the aluminium alloy ring used for identification of individuals in ecological studies. It slides freely along the forearm.

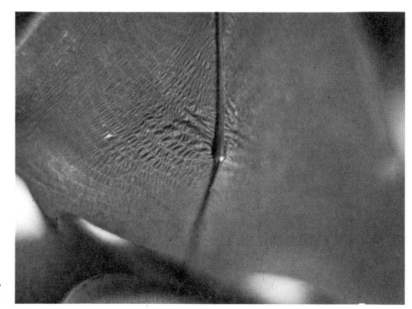

Juvenile metacarpal/finger joint in the wing. It keeps this gradually tapering appearance until the April after birth. By the second winter it becomes knobbly.

11

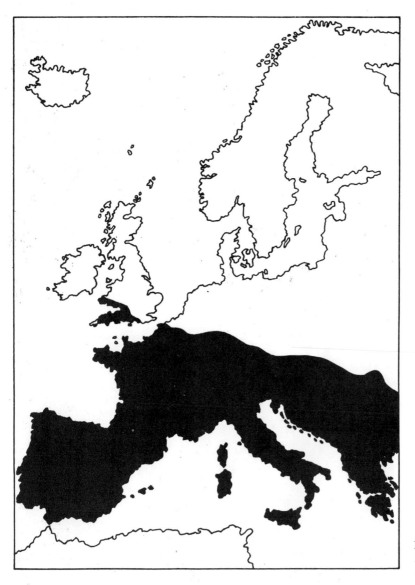

Fig. 2 *Distribution of the greater horseshoe bat in Europe. The black areas show the regions in which the species is capable of surviving naturally. Over much of this range it is rare, or virtually extinct.*

In Britain it is found only in hilly areas in caves and disused mines in the south west. One small population lives in Pembrokeshire, and others are found in Devon, Dorset, Somerset, Avon and Gloucestershire. Since serious studies of their numbers have only been started in the last twenty-five years, we have no clear idea of long term changes. However, museum records show that the bat's range has shrunk, probably due to the loss of suitable habitats. In Dorset, where an estimated 1,500 bats were present in the late 1950's, closure of many of the disused stone mines probably caused the serious fall in bat numbers to about 150.

Habitat
The kind of place this bat needs is affected by its supply of food. It can only afford to keep itself warm if it has a lot to eat. Without food it will starve to death in a few days if it is kept in a warm place. It chooses a cool place and lets its body temperature drop to the air level whenever food is in short supply to minimise the amount of energy used to stay alive.

In spring and summer, breeding females choose old houses or barns with suitable warm attics. The building must have some cellars or possibly a cave nearby, so that the bats can quickly move to a low temperature if insects are scarce. When the weather is warm, and insects are plentiful, they cluster in large active bunches in the attics. If a sudden cold spell occurs they move into the cellars or caves and become inactive. We call this state of temporary inactivity the torpid state.

In autumn and winter they start to hibernate in cellars, tunnels, caves and disused mines, as long as these places provide the right temperature. The best places offer a range of temperatures from 6 to 12°C, as this allows the bats to choose the exact level they need.

Conditions outside the cave are also important as they often feed during the hibernation period. Steep sided, south-facing slopes with mixed cattle pastures and hedgerows or copses as windbreaks, seem to produce the best conditions.

Front view of hanging bat.

 Besides providing the right temperatures, caves and other similar places supply total darkness and very damp air. The first protects the bats from predators, and the second stops the wings from drying out.

15

Early and late in the hibernation period small caves, mines, tunnels or cellars are used by adult males as breeding territories. These places are often too cold in mid-winter, and the bats abandon them for the larger caves at that time. This is why peak numbers occur in these caves during January and February. During mild winters they may remain spread out in the smaller sites.

Wherever they are, they need protection from repeated disturbance. They usually abandon caves that are regularly visited by caving groups.

Field Signs
Droppings and parts of insects are the best guide to the presence of bats in a cave. They usually collect near the entrance where a suitable dark vertical rift occurs. The rift should have a ridge on which the bats can cluster after feeding. Droppings average 5-6 mm long, and 2.5 mm wide. They vary from black to brown according to the food eaten.

The insect remains found in caves are likely to be from the dor beetle or the cockchafer. Usually only the abdomen has been eaten, and the rest falls to the ground.

Behaviour
The study of any nocturnal animal is not easy, and the study of one which flies is even more difficult. However, when hibernating they are easy to catch once their sites have been discovered.

The first studies on the greater horseshoe bat were carried out by John and Winnifred Hooper in Devon caves. They began to put rings on their forearms in 1948 so that they could trace their movements, and find out how long they live. I began a similar ringing study in

1956, and included a breeding population from 1959. By visiting a large number of different hibernation sites in four different counties around Bristol for more than twenty years, it has been possible to find out quite a lot about the behaviour of these bats. In addition I have made hundreds of visits to the breeding site in Gloucestershire to watch, and count the bats as they flew out to feed. On many occasions I have used an ultrasonic receiver to help trace the bats.

The bats fly very close to the ground or vegetation, and can reach speeds of 30 km/hour (8.3 m/s, or 17 mph). They are very agile, and can twist and turn to catch insects or avoid branches, with the help of their ultrasonic navigation. At close range you can hear the wing membranes flap during sharp turns. It is very much like an umbrella being shaken.

As the bats leave the building to feed, each one tends to travel in the same direction, at the same height. It is almost as if they have paths in the air. The farther they travel from the building, the less they keep to the same route, and they are soon very difficult to follow. Feeding exits last about half an hour, with a steady trickle of bats leaving on their own. When the numbers build up to 150 or 200 in July and August, small groups of bats may stream out together, but it is impossible to tell whether they follow one another to feed.

They only leave the building for about an hour, so they cannot travel farther than about 15 km (9 miles). Where they stop to feed, if they do so, still has not been discovered. They spend the night back in the attic, and go out again to feed for an hour before dawn.

During winter they commonly move 10 km (6 miles) between hibernation quarters, and even up to 20 km (12 miles) can be recorded. Longer movements than this may take place between summer and winter sites. The maximum distance moved of about 64 km (40 miles) has

Greater horseshoe in hibernation.

Flying bat at the end of its upstroke. Like a swimmer using butterfly stroke, the wings are ready to move downwards.

Flying bat in early downstroke. By grasping a 'handful of air' and pushing it backwards, the bat propels itself forwards.

19

been recorded by Hooper and myself, and appears to be the limit.

Feeding

If insect food is plentiful the bats can catch a stomach full in the one hour feeding period. This represents 4.5 g of insects, or 25% of the body weight per meal. With two meals per day, it means they eat 50%, or half their body weight per day in summer. Actually, since they only eat the softer parts of large insects, they catch more than this.

Their diet is difficult to discover, since the best way is to examine the droppings under a microscope which take a long time to analyse. It looks as if they feed on dung beetles and cockchafers in spring, then change to large moths in June, July and early August. Finally they switch back to dung beetles and also daddy long legs (crane flies) in late August and September. In winter they feed mostly on dung beetles.

Young bats seem to prefer the small brown dung beetles *(Aphodius)* when they first start to feed. Adults concentrate upon the large dor beetle *(Geotrupes)* which they often catch whilst it is still on the ground. The beetle makes a loud buzz as it tries to take off, and the bat is attracted to it and lands on it. Within a second or two the bat springs back into the air with the beetle in its mouth. The insect is so large that the bat has to hang up to deal with it. Often the bat returns to the building or cave from which it came so the remains collect there. Smaller prey are eaten more or less completely. Whatever is eaten, it is chewed very thoroughly, and any large lumps are stored in cheek pouches until it is ready for them.

Few insects are able to fly if the air temperature falls much below 10°C. This normally happens in late

October as the days shorten, and in April or May it rises back above 10°C, at least in the daytime. Temperature varies a lot from year to year so the bats have to be adaptable. Warm spells in winter allow those bats which have a shortage of stored fat to feed and avoid starvation.

Activity

The activity pattern of this bat is very variable. It depends upon many things, but the food supply is the most important aspect. The following list shows what a bat may do at any one time:

1. It can fly to feed or travel. Its body temperature (B.T.) reaches 41°C.
2. It can rest and keep warm at 37°C B.T.
3. It can rest and keep warm at 33°C B.T.
4. It can rest and switch off its B.T. control so that it cools to the same temperature as the air. If the air temperature is below 20°C it becomes inactive, or torpid. It wakes up every day.
5. It can rest in a cave in an air temperature of between 5 and 10°C when it will stay torpid for up to 10 days. Eventually it wakes at dusk. This is the hibernation state, and it only happens between October and early May.

The list is put in order of energy use. Flying is the most expensive, and hibernation is the least expensive. Over six hundred times as much energy is used in flight, compared with hibernation. It is only worth flying and trying to digest the catch if reasonable numbers of insects can be caught. By clustering together, the bats help each other to save heat whilst digesting their meal.

When it is torpid or hibernating the bat's heart beat falls to 10 or 15 beats per minute, compared with about 700 during flight. Its breathing rate also falls, and

The author weighing a bat. Note the helmet, cap lamp and boiler suit for safe caving, and the net used to reach torpid bats.

Cluster of 35 bats in a cellar in May, starting to arouse at dusk. Coloured rings were used so that bats could be aged and sexed without waking them up.

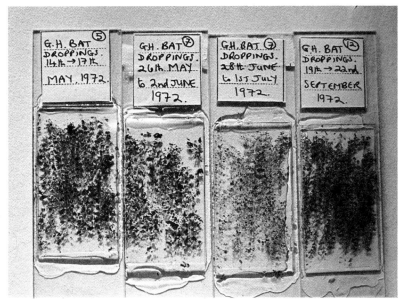

Microscope slides of bat droppings collected in 1972 from beneath the breeding cluster in an attic. Note the change in diet shown by colour differences.

becomes uneven. Fat is stored for hibernation in late September and October. One bat, which was born in July, increased from 17 to 24 g in 13 days. The extra weight was fat, which was used to survive the winter. If a bat has not stored enough fat by the end of October, it will feed later on during hibernation. Fat bats lose more weight than thin bats, so they all tend to weigh the same in spring.

Unlike many other hibernators, bats are very sensitive to being disturbed whilst hibernating. A torch light, or the slightest touch, is enough to make them wake up. First they bend their knees, and later on they begin to shiver. Finally their ears begin to twitch as they navigate before flying off.

By the spring individual bats have lost from one quarter to one third of their October weight, and must feed again or starve. Cold wet April and May weather causes many deaths, particularly in first year bats.

Social Structure

These bats do not just fly to any cave, or mine, to hibernate, even if the temperature conditions are right. There seem to be three main types of cave. The first is mainly occupied by first year bats with a few second years; the second has bats aged from two to six years, and the last is the territory of an adult male. He is visited by a number of adult females for short periods in October, November and April. Mating seems to occur at these times. Up to twenty different females may be found with a particular male over several winters.

In summer the breeding females gather together in the breeding site and adult males are not admitted. After weaning, the young are abandoned by their mothers early in September. The young stay in the breeding site until October, with a few second year bats which may act as guides for feeding or finding the caves.

Communication

Baby bats make high pitched squeaks if they are disturbed. These are distress signals to the mother who may return to collect it. Mothers call to their young when they return from feeding, and seem to identify their own baby from a mass of others.

When two hundred or more bats are crammed into a narrow space squabbles develop. Tape recordings taken from the attic after dusk and dawn, as the bats return from feeding, show that these are noisy times. Lots of wing flapping, baby distress calls and adult chirps can be heard as the group settles down for the day. By mid-afternoon everything is quiet. It seems likely that signals will occur to stop serious fights during the return period. Whatever they are, we do not know at present. Neither do we have any understanding of the way in which a male manages to hold on to a territory for ten years or longer.

Breeding

Adult males, like all mammals, make sperms in the reproductive organs, called testes. This can only happen in the summer when the bats can afford to keep themselves warm all the time. The sperms are then stored until the mating period which starts in late September, and is most common up to Christmas. Adult females begin hibernation in the male's territory, and he often starts to mate whilst she is still torpid. He lands above her and mates from behind, often chewing the fur at the back of her neck. Mating may last for three-quarters of an hour, by which time she is fully active.

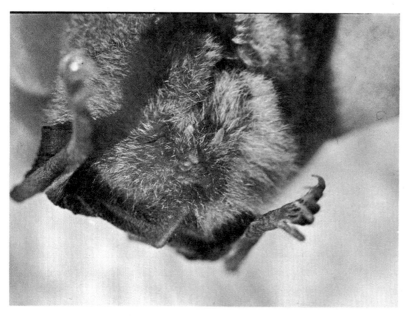

View of an adult breeding female to show the false teats projecting from the fur in the groin. The teats act as dummies when the young are not suckling.

Dried vaginal plugs collected from a polythene sheet spread on the floor of an attic in late April. They prove the attic was used by breeding females at that time.

A very young juvenile, four to five days old. Its eyes are shut, although the rest of the head is well developed. The forearms are short, pink and quite rubbery. It is solitary in the roost.

Daddy long legs (crane fly) resting in a field. These weak fliers are easily caught by young bats during September when they emerge from pupae in the ground.

After mating, a plug of gristle forms inside the female and stops any further mating. The sperms are stored inside her body until April, when the plug is pushed out, and fertilization of her egg occurs. Only one egg is made by the female, so only one young develops inside her body.

Although only one young is born per mother, it is very large. It weighs about 6 g at birth, or about 30% of the mother's weight. Birth occurs in mid July normally, but can be as late as early August. This long pregnancy, lasting three months or more, is due to periods when the mother became torpid because she could not feed properly. A house mouse, which is a similar weight, gives birth after 19 or 20 days.

Newly born bats are pink with short grey fur on the back, and rubbery finger bones. The wings are small, but the feet are nearly fully grown, with strong claws for gripping the roost. The face is quite well formed, but the eyes are closed. They grow very quickly and weigh 12 g when they are about 10 days old. The eyes are just open, and they begin making ultrasonic sounds. At 21 days old they weigh 15 to 16 g and are able to fly. Their forearms are about 5.0 cm long, compared with their mother's which are 5.4 cm. They then begin to fly out of the building to feed.

Suckling on milk made in the mother's two mammary glands lasts for four to five weeks, and insect feeding overlaps it. When first born the baby bats are left by their mothers, usually spaced out well away from the main group. As they get older the young group together to keep warm while their mothers are out feeding. They grip tightly to any object if their feet are removed from the roost. Very few babies die from falling unless heavy rain prevents their mothers from feeding. They probably become weak from starvation, since their mothers cannot produce milk without food.

It normally takes three years for baby bats to become sexually mature and breed. Males are able to breed before females, but since they rarely have a territory until they are four or five, they probably do not have a chance to mate.

Life Span

Ringing studies have shown that both male and female bats can live for over 20 years. The oldest bat I have caught was at least 22 years old, and a female of 19 years old was caught in the breeding site having recently given birth. If a bat reaches the age of 7 or 8 years, it has a very high survival rate. For adult females it is over 80% survival from one winter to the next. Most deaths occur in the first winter, or when the females first breed.

Predators and Mortality

Very few predators feed on bats in this country. Nearly all my records of predator deaths are from the owners of cats which have brought home a dead, ringed bat. The cats had probably caught the bats as they flew low to catch insects from the ground. One cave in Somerset had a family of cats which gained some of their food from catching bats as they flew up through a narrow entrance. They killed at least eight ringed bats in one winter. Only the chewed remains of the wing bones were left.

Cars also cause deaths, as the bats fly at just the right height for a collision. Several records of ringed bats being squashed into the radiator grilles of cars have been sent in. One bat which was found dead in a Basingstoke street, was almost certainly carried this way, as it had been ringed near Bath not long before.

Large groups of bats on cave roofs.

A juvenile nearly capable of flight, aged twelve to fourteen days. Its eyes are open and its forearms are nearly fully grown. At this age juveniles form excitable groups.

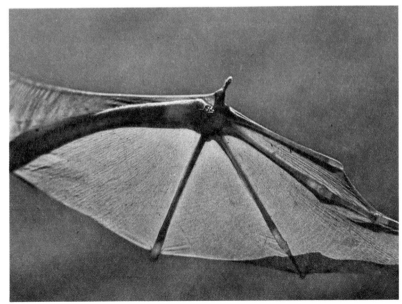

A juvenile wing showing the bright cartilage (gristle) gaps at the joints. The gaps allow the bones to grow to full size.

Only one case of damage caused by owls has been seen, and I know of no cases where their bones have been found in owl pellets.

Starvation at the end of long and severe winters seems to be the main cause of death, especially in first year bats. Very old bats may die of old age, since several have been found over many winters and shown a remarkably steady weight pattern until their last winter. One was found hanging up, having recently died despite having no signs of injuries.

Diseases are very rare, and they usually recover from serious injuries, including broken bones and torn wings, as long as the main arm bones are not damaged. One bat had most of the fur and skin of its underside ripped off in some way, yet lasted from October to April without apparent change. It reappeared the next October with a brand new bald skin!

A most unusual death was recorded one year, when an adult male was found dead beneath the breeding cluster in late May. He had half his face bitten away, and his arm muscles were badly chewed. It seemed certain from his injuries, and from his position, that he had been attacked by the females.

Relations with Man

Few people have successfully kept this bat as a pet, as it is a difficult thing to do. It is now illegal to try to keep them without a special licence. Unless the right temperature conditions can be provided it needs a lot of attention, and eats too much food. Mealworms can be provided as food, but they cost as much as caviar! If the bats are kept active in a warm room they need up to 10 g of mealworms per day. In fact mealworms alone are not enough to keep the bat healthy, and extra vitamins are needed.

Bats have both benefited and suffered from man's activities. Before man began mining for different materials the greater horseshoe must have been found only in areas with natural caves. The fact that they now exist in Gloucestershire, Wiltshire and Dorset is entirely due to the presence of disused mines, and suitable old buildings. A single mine represents an enormous cost in both human labour and money. Mines are also part of our history, and as time passes more people are interested in them as part of our industrial archaeology. Unfortunately if mines are not maintained they become dangerous places to anyone who acts foolishly inside them. The entrance regions, where frost action can loosen rocks, are especially dangerous. Because of this many disused mines have been filled in deliberately to make them safe. Others have rubbish dumped in them over a period of years so that eventually the air flow is stopped, and the mine becomes useless for hibernation.

The major increase in interest in caving, which seems likely to continue, has meant that many caves are now constantly visited. Some caves in Somerset have parties queuing up waiting for a turn to go down at weekends. No matter how careful the parties are at avoiding disturbance, the bats are often awakened. They gradually desert such caves, and so lose further hibernation sites. Their problems are increased by the tendency to repair old buildings, especially if powerful poisons are used to kill wood boring beetles. Breeding clusters have been badly affected by this kind of treatment.

It seems likely that the serious decline in the numbers of bats of this species since the 1950's was due to all these effects, together with the loss of food. Insect populations fell greatly after the use of insecticides, and with a series of long cold winters in the mid-1960's many bats starved.

Juveniles parked in an attic after the exit of their mothers to feed. Because of its large size, the mother does not carry her single young out to feed.

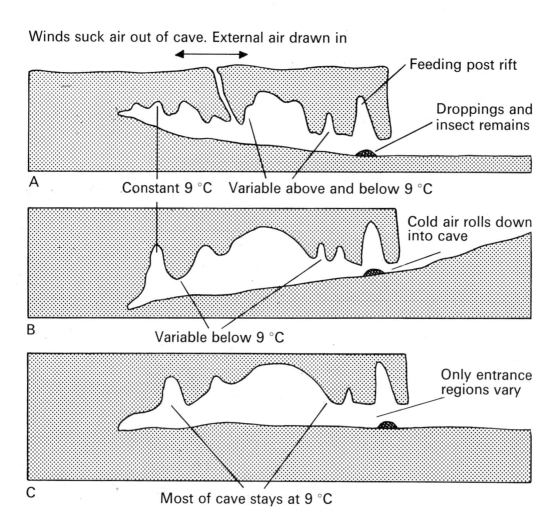

Winds suck air out of cave. External air drawn in

Feeding post rift

Droppings and insect remains

A Constant 9 °C   Variable above and below 9 °C

Cold air rolls down into cave

B Variable below 9 °C

Only entrance regions vary

C Most of cave stays at 9 °C

Fig. 3 *Cave types classified according to the temperatures available for hibernation. Only variable temperature caves are used throughout hibernation.*

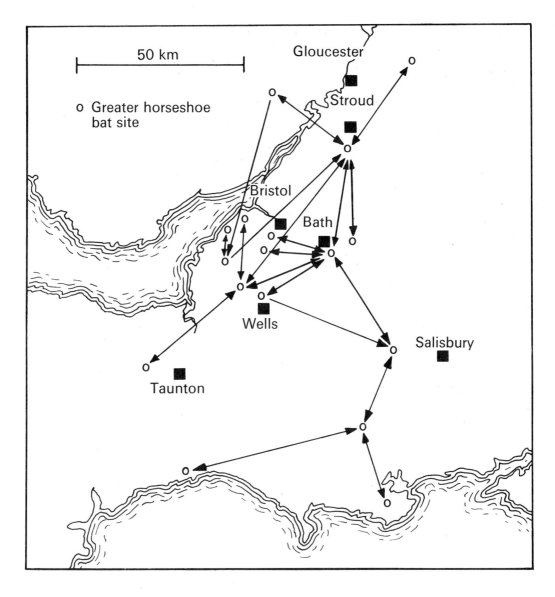

Fig. 4 *Some major movements recorded over a 20 year study period. Such movements are rare, and most bats remain within 25 miles (40 km) of their birthplace.*

Close-ups of bats in flight.

A bat, which died at the end of its first winter, being decomposed by fungi whilst still suspended. It died of starvation during April.

A dead bat which has been decomposed to its skeleton in the humid atmosphere of a cave.

39

Conservation

I believe that this animal, like all other British bats, deserves a place in this country. It is an extremely interesting creature showing many unusual features in its structure, behaviour and breeding. Popular ideas about bats, which come from Dracula films and cartoon strips, are very inaccurate and misleading. If we can protect every species of British bird, and spend huge sums of money on them every year, surely we cannot allow our bats to be lost.

What do we need to do in order to ensure their survival? We must set aside enough breeding and hibernation sites for a reasonable population to be able to live successfully. Certain caves and mines need to be listed and kept for hibernation between late September and early May. Human access could be allowed at other times. This means that the entrances to such places must be gated so that human entrance can be control-led. The gates must not alter the flow of air into the site, since the temperatures inside will alter and the bats will not use it.

A start has already been made on this work, aided by the Nature Conservancy Council and some of the County Naturalists Trusts. Dr R. E. Stebbings has been especially active in this work throughout the country, encouraging local groups to do the work. Unfortunately money for doing it is not easy to obtain, and a single entrance may cost £150 to gate, even with voluntary labour. Some large entrances are impossible to protect.

Since the Conservation of Wild Creatures and Wild Plants Act of 1975, the law has protected this bat. You are not allowed to disturb, ring or keep one in captivity without a licence. However, this does not stop land-owners from filling in old mines, or renovating their old buildings.

Having fallen to about one half of their late 1950's

level, the numbers of bats caught recently have risen. This may have been due to a series of mild winters, or to the protection of about ten of the most important sites. Only time will tell which of these two was more important.

Entrance to a cave which has been grilled to protect the bats from disturbance during hibernation. Note the removable gate and the notice informing readers of the reasons for the grille.